KNOCK UPON SILENCE

KNOCK UPON SILENCE

Poems by Carolyn Kizer

We wrestle with non-being
to force it to yield up being;
we knock upon silence
for an answering music. . . .

FROM THE *Wên-Fu* OF LU CHI

UNIVERSITY OF WASHINGTON PRESS
Seattle and London

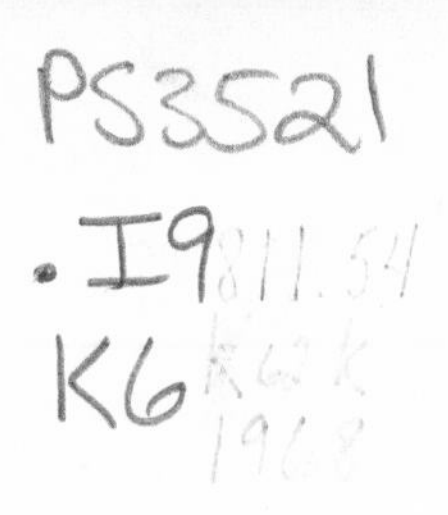

CHINESE IMITATIONS: The poems in Part I have appeared *The Spectator* (London) and also in *Shenandoah* and *Choice.*

A MONTH IN SUMMER appeared in *The Kenyon Review* and *E counter.*

The three sections of PRO FEMINA appeared in *The Carleton M cellany.*

TU FU: *Déjeuner sur L'Herbe, Lo Yu Park* (under the title of *Th Tourist Park*), and *Thwarted* appeared in *Poetry; The Meanderin River Poems* in *The Kenyon Review,* and the nine remaining poem in *The Hudson Review.*

TESTAMENT appeared in *Sewanee Review.*

Published by arrangement with Doubleday & Company, Inc.

Library of Congress Catalog Card Number 65-19901
Washington Paperback edition, 1968
Printed in the United States of America

ACKNOWLEDGMENTS

I have been reading the poetry of Arthur Waley since childhood, and, like so many of my contemporaries, my debt and my devotion to him is incalculable. I am grateful to Nobuyuki Yuasa for his superb translation of Issa's *The Year of My Life* (University of California Press), which gave me the form for *A Month in Summer,* and also provided me with the most satisfactory method of writing *haiku.* Another debt acknowledged by a dedication is to Rolfe Humphries and Robert Fitzgerald, my friends: without the example of the former and the encouragement of the latter, *Pro Femina* would have perished in a notebook.

For Tu Fu, the debts are many: first, to Donald Keene, who incited me; second, to Cyril Birch, who chastised me, praised me and laughed at me (and who bears no responsibility for errors and embroideries which their author insists on regarding as felicities); third, to William Hung, without whose edition of the life and works of Tu Fu (Harvard), I would have been helpless indeed.

But I must single out Donald Keene, whose mind and friendship are the crown of my life and the support of what art I possess.

C.A.K.

West Pakistan, 1965

CONTENTS

I. *CHINESE IMITATIONS* 1

For Jan, in Bar Maria 3
Singing Aloud 4
Amusing Our Daughters 6
Hiding Our Love 8
Night Sounds 9
Summer Near the River 11
The Skein 13
Winter Song 14

II. *A MONTH IN SUMMER* 17

III. *from PRO FEMINA* 39

One 41
Two 44
Three 47

IV. *Translations of TU FU* 51

Déjeuner sur L'Herbe 53
Lo Yu Park 55
The Meandering River Poems 58
Rain There 58
Drinking with Friends 60
Drinking There Alone 61
Spring Goes 62
I Go Too 63
Thwarted 64
Adviser to the Court 67
East of the Palace Gates: Working Late 67
To a Brother Official 69
Working All Night in Springtime 70
End of an Audience 71
Reply to a Friend's Advice 72
On the Way Out 73
Banishment 74
Too Much Heat, Too Much Work 74
Reunion 75
A Visit in Winter 76
Testament 79

I

CHINESE IMITATIONS

FOR ARTHUR WALEY, IN HOMAGE

FOR JAN, IN BAR MARIA

Though it's true we were young girls when we met,
We have been friends for twenty-five years.
But we still swim strongly, run up the hill from the beach
without getting too winded.
Here we idle in Ischia, a world away from our birthplace—
That colorless town!—drinking together, sisters of summer.
Now we like to have groups of young men gathered around
us.
We are trivial-hearted. We don't want to die any more.

Remember, fifteen years ago, in our twin pinafores
We danced on the boards of the ferry dock at Mukilteo
Mad as yearling mares in the full moon?
Here in the morning moonlight we climbed on a workman's
cart
And three young men, shouting and laughing, dragged it up
through the streets of the village.
It is said we have shocked the people of Forio.
They call us Janna and Carolina, those two mad *straniere*.

SINGING ALOUD

We all have our faults. Mine is trying to write poems.
New scenery, someone I like, anything sets me off!
I hear my own voice going on, like a god or an oracle,
That cello-tone, intuition. That bell-note of wisdom!

And I can't get rid of the tempting tic of pentameter,
Of the urge to impose a form on what I don't understand,
Or that which I have to transform because it's too grim as
it is.
But age is improving me: Now, when I finish a poem

I no longer rush out to impose it on friendly colleagues.
I climb through the park to the reservoir, peer down at my
own reflection,
Shake a blossoming branch so I am covered with petals,
Each petal a metaphor. . . .

By the time we reach middle life, we've all been deserted and
robbed.
But flowers and grass and animals keep me warm.
And I remind myself to become philosophic:
We are meant to be stripped down, to prepare us for
something better.

And, often, I sing aloud. As I grow older
I give way to innocent folly more and more often.
The squirrels and rabbits chime in with inaudible voices.
I feel sure that the birds make an effort to be antiphonal.

When I go to the zoo, the primates and I, in communion,
Hoot at each other, or signal with earthy gestures.
We must move further out of town, we musical birds and
animals,
Or they'll lock us up like the apes, and control us forever.

AMUSING OUR DAUGHTERS

for Robert Creeley

We don't lack people here on the Northern coast,
But they are people one meets, not people one cares for.
So I bundle my daughters into the car
And with my brother poets, go to visit you, brother.

Here come your guests! A swarm of strangers and children;
But the strangers write verses, the children are daughters like
  yours.
We bed down on mattresses, cots, roll up on the floor:
Outside, burly old fruit trees in mist and rain;
In every room, bundles asleep like larvae.

We waken and count our daughters. Otherwise, nothing
happens.
You feed them sweet rolls and melon, drive them all to the
zoo;
Patiently, patiently, ever the father, you answer their
questions.
Later we eat again, drink, listen to poems.
Nothing occurs, though we are aware you have three
daughters
Who last year had four. But even death becomes part of our
ease:
Poems, parenthood, sorrow, all we have learned
From these, of tenderness, holds us together
In the center of life, entertaining daughters
By firelight, with cake and songs.

You, my brother, are a good and violent drinker,
Good at reciting short-line or long-line poems.
In time we will lose all our daughters, you and I,
Be temperate, venerable, content to stay in one place,
Sending our messages over the mountains and waters.

HIDING OUR LOVE

Never believe I leave you
From any desire to go.
Never believe I live so far away
Except from necessity.
After a whole day of separation
Still your dark fragrance clings to my skin.
I carry your letter everywhere.
The sash of my dress wraps twice around my waist.
I wish it bound the two of us together.

Do you know that we both conceal our love
Because of prior sorrow, superstitious fear?
We are two citizens of a savage era
Schooled in disguises and in self-command,
Hiding our aromatic, vulnerable love.

NIGHT SOUNDS

The moonlight on my bed keeps me awake;
Living alone now, aware of the voices of evening,
A child weeping at nightmares, the faint love-cries of a
woman,
Everything tinged by terror or nostalgia.

No heavy, impassive back to nudge with one foot
While coaxing, "Wake up and hold me,"
When the moon's creamy beauty is transformed
Into a map of impersonal desolation.

But, restless in this mock dawn of moonlight
That so chills the spirit, I alter our history:
You were never able to lie quite peacefully at my side,
Not the night through. Always withholding something.

Awake before morning, restless and uneasy,
Trying not to disturb me, you would leave my bed
While I lay there rigidly, feigning sleep.
Still—the night was nearly over, the light not as cold
As a full cup of moonlight.

And there were the lovely times when, to the skies' cold *No*
You cried to me, *Yes!* Impaled me with affirmation.
Now when I call out in fear, not in love, there is no answer.
Nothing speaks in the dark but the distant voices,
A child with the moon on his face, a dog's hollow cadence.

SUMMER NEAR THE RIVER

I have carried my pillow to the windowsill
And try to sleep, with my damp arms crossed upon it
But no breeze stirs the tepid morning.
Only I stir. . . . Come, tease me a little!
With such cold passion, so little teasing play,
How long can we endure our life together?

No use. I put on your long dressing-gown;
The untied sash trails over the dusty floor.
I kneel by the window, prop up your shaving mirror
And pluck my eyebrows.
I don't care if the robe slides open
Revealing a crescent of belly, a tan thigh.
I can accuse that non-existent breeze. . . .

I am as monogamous as the North Star
But I don't want you to know it. You'd only take advantage.
While you are as fickle as spring sunlight.
All right, sleep! The cat means more to you than I.
I can rouse you, but then you swagger out.
I glimpse you from the window, striding towards the river.

When you return, reeking of fish and beer,
There is salt dew in your hair. Where have you been?
Your clothes weren't that wrinkled hours ago, when you left.
You couldn't have loved someone else, after loving me!
I sulk and sigh, dawdling by the window.
Later, when you hold me in your arms
It seems, for a moment, the river ceases flowing.

THE SKEIN

Moonlight through my gauze curtains
Turns them to nets for snaring wild birds,
Turns them into woven traps, into shrouds.
The old, restless grief keeps me awake.
I wander around, holding a scarf or shawl;
In the muffled moonlight I wander around
Folding it carefully, shaking it out again.
Everyone says my old lover is happy.
I wish they said he was coming back to me.
I hesitate here, my scarf like a skein of yarn
Binding my two hands loosely
        that would reach for paper and pen.

So I memorize these lines,
Dew on the scarf, dappling my nightdress also.
O love long gone, it is raining in our room!
So I memorize these lines,
        without salutation, without close.

WINTER SONG

on a line from Arthur Waley

So I go on, tediously on and on. . . .
We are separated, finally, not by death but life.
We cling to the dead, but the living break away.

On my birthday, the waxwings arrive in the garden,
Strip the trees bare as my barren heart.
I put out suet and bread for December birds:
Hung from evergreen branches, greasy gray
Ornaments for the rites of the winter solstice.

How can you and I meet face to face
After our triumphant love?
After our failure?

Since this isolation, it is always cold.
My clothes don't fit. My hair refuses to obey.
And, for the first time, I permit
These little anarchies of flesh and object.
Together, they flick me towards some final defeat.

Thinking of you, I am suddenly old. . . .
A mute spectator as the months wind by.
I have tried to put you out of my mind forever.

Home isn't here. It went away with you,
Disappearing in the space of a breath,
In the time one takes to open a foreknown letter.
My fists are bruised from beating on the ground.
There are clouds between me and the watery light.

Truly, I try to flourish, to find pleasure
Without an endless reference to you
Who made the days and years seem worth enduring.

II

A MONTH IN SUMMER

A MONTH IN SUMMER

First Day:

Several years ago, I wrote *haiku* in this way:

The frost was late this year:
Crystal nips the petals
As my lover grows impatient.

I have come to prefer the four-line form which Nobuyuki Yuasa has used in translating Issa because, as he says, it comes closer to approximating the natural rhythm of English speech:

Let down the curtain!
Hamlet dies each night
But is always revived.
Love, too, requires genius.

Perhaps that can stand, also, as my attempt to put, "O my prophetic soul!" into *haiku*.

Second Day:

The drama of love:
Scenes, intermissions
Played by two actors,
Their own spectators.

Third Day:

Strange how the tedium of love makes women babble, while it reduces men to a dour silence. As my voice skipped along the surfaces of communication like a water-bug, below it I sensed his quiet: the murky depths of the pond.

Alone, I play a Telemann concerto on the phonograph. A rather pedantic German note on the slip-case speaks of, "the curious, upward-stumbling theme." Can we be upward-stumbling? If so, there is hope for us.

When you go away
I play records till dawn
To drown the echoes
Of my own voice.

Fourth Day:

As a reaction from trying to please, one becomes
reckless and resentful:

Lights in every room.
I turned on more!
You sat with one hand
Shading your eyes.

Fifth Day:

I listen to myself being deliberately annoying,
deliberately irritating. I know so well, now,
what he hates; I can so easily provoke it.
It is a kind of furious attempt to rouse us both
from the inert boredom with which we regard our
life together. I'd like to sting him into madness,
as if I were one of the Erinyes. I don't believe
he is capable of understanding why I behave this way.

Sixth Day:

A party at which we play our customary roles. Later,
when the guests go home, he says, "Let's have a
serious talk." Invariably, he wants to have
elaborate discussions only when I am dead with fatigue,
and incapable of listening or responding. So I beg off.
Reckless, impatient, I hurry him away.

Seventh Day:

Some friends come to visit for a few hours.
My daughter Laurel picked roses for them, dozen
after dozen, until the garden was stripped of
ripening flowers. It was a relatively easy winter.
The aphids seemed to be under control this year.
One must not allow one's self to become superstitious
about the tremendous, massive florescence of roses,
nor about the great numbers of pregnant women.
It doesn't necessarily mean that the days of the world
are numbered; merely that the life-impulse is putting
forth an extra effort, just in case.

Eighth Day:

We agree not to see each other for a while. Now for a period of bravado, while we pretend that we have no need for that total, mutual dependence which has been habitual for so long.

Ninth Day:

Sometimes it's best to run away for a little.

Tenth Day:

I decided to return the visit of my friends. So, with my two daughters, I drove south. When we arrived, we saw the flowers Laurel had picked for them three days earlier. We had packed the masses of roses—white, yellow, and heat-faded pink—into a ten-gallon jar. The bouquet is still a large, fresh globe, in spite of the warmth of a four-hour drive, and the passing of thirsty days.

Roses should always
Rest in glass containers
Revealing the pattern
Of packed thorns and stems.

How happy one can seem—even to one's self—in the presence of others!

Eleventh Day:

On the porch two squirrels,
Half-grown and chubby,
Play at making love.
And we parents smile.

Twelfth Day:

In the afternoon, my daughters and my father and I
go out on a friend's boat, to the river that seems
as vast as a sea. My old father stays in the cabin
while the rest of the adults brace their feet on the
deck and drink the spray. Laurel, eleven, sits inside
with him and takes his hand, and says, "Are you all
right, grandpa?" I am touched by her gentle and
tactful solicitude. And I reflect that there is a
difference of over seventy years in their ages.

Thirteenth Day:

We came home last night. I drove slowly, with a cargo of two sleeping children. After they were in bed, I took presents to his house, as it was his birthday. But it looked as if he had retired for the night, so I left the gifts on the screen-porch.

> The shadow of leaves
> On your door, at night. . . .
> I'm a young girl again,
> Tip-toeing home.

The pattern of the maple, etched by the street lamp shining against the side of his house reminded me of my own home, years ago. The silhouettes of leaves and whip-like branches of our old white birch would be flickering on the porch when I came home late and alone. Perhaps, too, that same sense of desolation I felt then: a young girl in a small town, without congenial friends, with ageing parents. Lovers as yet unmet, in the far-off cities of my imagination. . . .

Fourteenth Day:

He telephoned to ask if I would mind if he exchanged the present I had given him. I knew when I picked it out that he wouldn't care for it. Even in this perversity I'm not being original, but am behaving like every woman mismanaging every love affair on record. I suppose that what we want is to be given a cuff, and told to behave ourselves!

Fifteenth Day:

School is out for the summer. The children will be away for a few weeks, and I can concentrate all of my time and attention on being unhappy. One should always end a love-affair in summer, when one's social life is at an ebb, and the sun is shining. Sunlight provides the excuse for dark glasses to hide swollen eye-lids, and permits the important events of one's life to take place unwitnessed, as in Greek tragedy.

Alone in my house
I can make gross noises
Like a caught hare or stoat
Or a woman in labor.

Sixteenth Day:

Nearly every night I dream of my mother, dead these four years. I remember reading an account by a well-known doctor, himself the victim of the agonizing disease which had been his specialty, saying that in extreme pain we all call for our mothers.

> I dream of the dead,
> Kind, brilliant and comforting.
> The lost return to us
> When we are lost.

Seventeenth Day:

Inertia, planned and involuntary. Do things come to an end because we no longer have the energy to pursue them, or does the prescience of this ending drain us of energy?

Eighteenth Day:

The pleasure of pain:
It destroys pretension.
We abandon effort
And live lying down.

Nineteenth Day:

Inertia.

One of the profound consolations in reading the works of Japanese men of letters is their frank acknowledgment of neurotic sloth. Or the overwhelming impulse, when faced with hurt or conflict, to stay in bed under the covers!

Twentieth Day:

Make a gigantic effort. Surely there are at least three or four persons, out of the four hundred thousand inhabitants of this city, whom I would care to see.

Later: I drove out to visit two artist friends. One of them is painting butterbur, but isn't fond of the name of it. I am reminded of the episode in Issa's journal when an eleven-year-old priest named Takamaru slips while crossing a bridge, and is drowned. When his body is discovered, wedged between two rocks, "even the sleeves of those unused to weep were wet with tears when they discovered in his pocket a few blossoms of butterbur—just picked—perhaps intended as a happy present for his parents. . . ."

For G.
Your paintings of butterbur
Might be called, "Colt's Foot"
Or, simply, "Homage
To Takamaru."

That should be suitably obscure!

G. is angry and impatient with his work: "They just look *pretty* and *cheap!*" he storms, and has to be restrained from doing away with them.

You hate the paintings
Made with such love.
Not you who are mad
But a mad century!

Twenty-first Day:

Is it suffering which defeminizes? Or the sense
that one is relinquishing sexual love, perhaps
forever?

Neutered and wistful,
My spinster cat
Stands on my chest
And laps up my tears.

Each morning I am wakened by my own weeping, and
the rasp, rasp of the little cat's tongue
across my cheek.

Twenty-second Day:

I run across my friend on the street and we talk for a bit. He urges me into a nearby "greasy spoon" for a cup of coffee. We sit at a table smeared with food and cluttered with soiled dishes. A water-glass holds cigarette stubs and wet ashes. I am feeling quite faint. No one waits on us. I get up to run away, but he insists that I sit down again. We analyze, very calmly, very objectively, the faults we find in one another. How trivial they are! Idiotic! Don't we dare to broach the larger topics? And love—doesn't it endure somewhere peacefully, like an underground river, beneath all this dust and meaningless commotion on the surface?

However, we both seem relieved of some tension by this exchange, and part amiably.

Twenty-third Day:

No, I am *not*
A cricket in a matchbox,
Nor are you a boy,
To keep pets in your pocket.

We meet. We talk. And so? Nothing changes.

Twenty-fourth Day:

An acquaintance reproaches me: "You shouldn't give him up. The world is overrun with lost, lonely women. Make any compromise."

I am too arrogant to take something over nothing. But I well know that all my arrogance is going to be flayed out of me. I am going to be stripped and flayed of all of it. *He* doesn't know that he is going to do this to me; he protests violently when I tell him so. But I know it.

Twenty-fifth Day:

Strange how the range
Of possibility dwindles.
Imagination fails us
When we need her most.

There should be so many alternative courses of action. Instead, self-destruction becomes finally comprehensible.

The terror of loss:
Not the grief of a wet branch
In autumn, but the absolute
Arctic desolation.

One simply lies in the dark contemplating loss, as if it were luminous: in itself a kind of mystic experience.

Twenty-sixth Day:

Do I see him approaching? Instinctively, I flinch, duck my head, crook an arm across my face. I hurry past, and don't really know if he saw me or not.

Your handsomeness. I find it
An irrelevant fact
To file away carefully
For my old age.

The other day I caught a glimpse of him playing the pinball machine in the same coffee shop where we met last week. Are *his* days such a wasteland then?

Twenty-seventh Day:

Seen through tears
This moonlight
Is no more poignant
Than a saucer of cream.

Why the artifice of this *haibun,* which I have appropriated from a culture which doesn't belong to me? Perhaps to lose *me.* Perhaps because the only way to deal with sorrow is to find a form in which to contain it.

And, at last, surely it is time to study restraint?

Twenty-eighth Day:

A *tanka:*

I stayed up all night
Till the sky turned to saffron
Behind black mountains.

I saw the color of hell
Has its own kind of beauty.

Twenty-ninth Day:

I was playing the Telemann concerto over and over. I bought two copies and gave one to my friend. Now I am reduced to wondering whether we are listening to the same record at the same time of night.

The music I play
This summer and fall:
Will I hear it at sixty
And be ready to die?

Perhaps at the extremes of happiness or unhappiness, one should take care that only inferior works of art will be contaminated by nostalgia. And, after all, it is well known that a cheap popular song can arouse through its associations a more violent reaction than the greatest composition.

Thirtieth Day:

It's all over.

> I realize now
> The dialectic error:
> Not love against death,
> But hope, the bulwark.

Holding his letter, barely skimmed, in my hand, I drove to the house of my only intimate friend. She was not at home. I caught a glimpse of myself reflected in a window: a reeling ghost. Suddenly G., the artist, appeared before me. Though in ten years we've hardly exchanged a personal word, I took his hand and held it very tightly in both of mine, and he supported me along the street to my car.

Much later, at G.'s house, I saw the other copy of the Telemann, which I had given my friend, lying on the table. So the links are broken.

Nothing remains.

And the worst, unimaginable until now: it is as if nothing had ever been.

"Is that what is meant by dwelling in unreality? And here too I end my words."

III

from PRO FEMINA

FOR ROBERT AND ROLFE

ONE

From Sappho to myself, consider the fate of women.
How unwomanly to discuss it! Like a noose or an albatross
 necktie
The clinical sobriquet hangs us: cod-piece coveters.
Never mind these epithets; I myself have collected some
 honeys.
Juvenal set us apart in denouncing our vices
Which had grown, in part, from having been set apart:
Women abused their spouses, cuckolded them, even plotted
To poison them. Sensing, behind the violence of his
 manner—
"Think I'm crazy or drunk?"—his emotional stake in us,
As we forgive Strindberg and Nietzsche, we forgive all those
Who cannot forget us. We *are* hyenas. Yes, we admit it.

While men have politely debated free will, we have howled
for it,
Howl still, pacing the centuries, tragedy heroines.
Some who sat quietly in the corner with their embroidery
Were Defarges, stabbing the wool with the names of their
ancient
Oppressors, who ruled by the divine right of the male—
I'm impatient of interruptions! I'm aware there were millions
Of mutes for every Saint Joan or sainted Jane Austen,
Who, vague-eyed and acquiescent, worshiped God as a man.
I'm not concerned with those cabbageheads, not truly
feminine
But neutered by labor. I mean real women, like *you*
and like *me*.

Freed in fact, not in custom, lifted from furrow and scullery,
Not obliged, now, to be the pot for the annual chicken,
Have we begun to arrive in time? With our well-known
Respect for life because it hurts so much to come out with it;
Disdainful of "sovereignty," "national honor" and other
abstractions;

We can say, like the ancient Chinese to successive waves of
invaders,
"Relax, and let us absorb you. You can learn temperance
In a more temperate climate." Give us just a few decades
Of grace, to encourage the fine art of acquiescence
And we might save the race. Meanwhile, observe our
creative chaos,
Flux, efflorescence—whatever you care to call it!

TWO

I take as my theme, "The Independent Woman,"
Independent but maimed: observe the exigent neckties
Choking violet writers; the sad slacks of stipple-faced
matrons;
Indigo intellectuals, crop-haired and callous-toed,
Cute spectacles, chewed cuticles, aced out by full-time
beauties
In the race for a male. Retreating to drabness, bad manners
And sleeping with manuscripts. Forgive our transgressions
Of old gallantries as we hitch in chairs, light our own
cigarettes,
Not expecting your care, having forfeited it by trying to get
even.

But we need dependency, cosseting and well-treatment.
So do men sometimes. Why don't they admit it?
We will be cows for a while, because babies howl for us,
Be kittens or bitches, who want to eat grass now and then
For the sake of our health. But the role of pastoral heroine
Is not permanent, Jack. We want to get back to the meeting.

Knitting booties and brows, tartars or termagants, ancient
Fertility symbols, chained to our cycle, released
Only in part by devices of hygiene and personal daintiness,
Strapped into our girdles, held down, yet uplifted by man's
Ingenious constructions, holding coiffures in a breeze,
Hobbled and swathed in whimsey, tripping on feminine
Shoes with fool heels, losing our lipsticks, you, me,
In ephemeral stockings, clutching our handbags and
packages.

Our masks, always in peril of smearing or cracking,
In need of continuous check in the mirror or silverware,
Keep us in thrall to ourselves, concerned with our surfaces.
Look at man's uniform drabness, his impersonal envelope!
Over chicken wrists or meek shoulders, a formal, hard-fibered
assurance.
The drape of the male is designed to achieve self-
forgetfulness.

So, sister, forget yourself a few times and see where it gets
you:
Up the creek, alone with your talent, sans everything else.
You can wait for the menopause, and catch up on your
reading.
So primp, preen, prink, pluck and prize your flesh,
All posturings! All ravishment! All sensibility!
Meanwhile, have you used your mind today?
What pomegranate raised you from the dead,
Springing, full-grown, from your own head, Athena?

THREE

I will speak about women of letters, for I'm in the racket.
Our biggest successes to date? Old maids to a woman.
And our saddest conspicuous failures? The married
spinsters
On loan to the husbands they treated like surrogate fathers.
Think of that crew of self-pitiers, not-very-distant,
Who carried the torch for themselves and got first-degree
burns.
Or the sad sonneteers, toast-and-teasdales we loved at
thirteen;
Middle-aged virgins seducing the purile anthologists
Through lust-of-the-mind; barbiturate-drenched Camilles
With continuous periods, murmuring softly on sofas
When poetry wasn't a craft but a sickly effluvium,
The air thick with incense, musk, and emotional blackmail.

I suppose they reacted from an earlier womanly modesty
When too many girls were scabs to their stricken
 sisterhood,
Impugning our sex to stay in good with the men,
Commencing their insecure bluster. How they must have
 swaggered
When women themselves indorsed their own inferiority!
Vestals, vassals and vessels, rolled into several,
They took notes in rolling syllabics, in careful journals,
Aiming to please a posterity that despises them.
But we'll always have traitors who swear that a woman
 surrenders
Her Supreme Function, by equating Art with aggression
And failure with Femininity. Still, it's just as unfair
To equate Art with Femininity, like a prettily-packaged
 commodity
When we are the custodians of the world's best-kept secret:
Merely the private lives of one-half of humanity.

But even with masculine dominance, we mares and mistresses
Produced some sleek saboteuses, making their cracks
Which the porridge-brained males of the day were too
 thick to perceive,
Mistaking young hornets for perfectly harmless bumblebees.
Being thought innocuous rouses some women to frenzy;
They try to be ugly by aping the ways of the men
And succeed. Swearing, sucking cigars and scorching the
 bedspread,

Slopping straight shots, eyes blotted, vanity-blown
In the expectation of glory: *she writes like a man!*
This drives other women mad in a mist of chiffon
(one poetess draped her gauze over red flannels, a practical
feminist).

But we're emerging from all that, more or less,
Except for some lady-like laggards and Quarterly priestesses
Who flog men for fun, and kick women to maim competition.
Now, if we struggle abnormally, we may almost seem normal;
If we submerge our self-pity in disciplined industry;
If we stand up and be hated, and swear not to sleep with
editors;
If we regard ourselves formally, respecting our true
limitations
Without making an unseemly show of trying to unfreeze our
assets;
Keeping our heads and our pride while remaining unmarried;
And if wedded, kill guilt in its tracks when we stack up the
dishes
And defect to the typewriter. And if mothers, believe in the
luck of our children,
Whom we forbid to devour us, whom we shall not devour,
And the luck of our husbands and lovers, who keep
free women.

IV

TU FU

(A.D. 712–770)

TRANSLATIONS

FOR DONALD

DÉJEUNER SUR L'HERBE

I

It's pleasant to board the ferry in the sunscape
As the late light slants into afternoon;
The faint wind ruffles the river, rimmed with foam.
We move through the aisles of bamboo
Towards the cool water-lilies.

The young dandies drop ice into the drinks,
While the girls slice the succulent lotus root.
Above us, a patch of cloud spreads, darkening
Like a water-stain on silk.

Write this down quickly, before the rain!

II

Don't sit there! The cushions were soaked by the
shower.
Already the girls have drenched their crimson skirts.
Beauties, their powder streaked with mascara,
lament their ruined faces.

The wind batters our boat, the mooring-line
Has rubbed a wound in the willow bark.
The edges of the curtains are embroidered by river foam.
Like a knife in a melon, Autumn slices Summer.

It will be cold, going back.

LO YU PARK

freely adapted

An opulent park: serene, we chose the heights.
Here the horizon fades
And the bright grass goes on forever. . . .

Our hosts move consciously, aware they create the view,
themselves the foreground.
Aristocratic, darkly groomed: forms disposed on emerald
lawns.
Distant rivers, flat and shiny as freshly-painted landscape
flow into the ladies' shoulders,
Emerge like scarves the other side.
Sport with the women! Open the lavish hampers!
Guzzle the wine, gleaming and wet as rivers. . . .

Later, half-drunk, slung into saddles,
We are the slaves of horses that gallop away.
Passing the Princess' Pond, we lean over fondly,
Find Spring's young green reflection sobering.
Then, battered by drums from the covered passageway,
We move on.

The sun is free to enter the Palace yard.
The gate spreads wide, lured open by the sun.
There, where the river curls, we meet the chariots
Sun-plated in silver, moons below the sky.

Blinded by polished gleam, we are distracted
By dancers: their long sleeves dip towards the water.
Courting the water, their skirts tease.
Distracted, distracted: focus our concentration
On a song:
the singer's voice a thin wire spiraling
To the clouds. . . .

I always get drunk this time of year.
Spring and her melancholy—but now it's too long
Until the wine takes hold. I become so morose!
One doesn't achieve the pleasure any more,
Just the stupidity.
I query a half-draped girl:
Who could want this poor pedant with thin hair?
Not the Court, surely. God alone feeds me.
She is tawny from sun, she is half-turned away.
Other bodies recumbent: "Who cares for you?"
I don't mind how drunk I get. I'll take every dare,
Every forfeit. But I can't see beyond the party's end!
Stand alone in the landscape, a sanguine figure.

You, poet, make a song by yourself. Be lost in your song.

THE MEANDERING RIVER POEMS

Rain There

Spring clouds rest on the walls of the Royal Park.
Dusk mutes the passionate coloring of blossoms.
Enclosed by the forest, in the River Pavilion,
I look at painted petals, dark from rain.

The wind has extended the waterweeds
Into long, writhing forms:
Like girdles of pale jade, they are curling,
Uncurling on the surface of the stream.

Incense burns in the Hibiscus Hall,
The scent faint, to no purpose.
Where, then, is the irresistible chariot
Guarded by dragons and Imperial tigers?

O King, return! Be liberal with your money!
Revive those elegant Royal entertainments
So I may doze, my old head tilted back
Against a tipsy old brocaded wall

While suave, accomplished ladies
Pluck at my sleeve, as they touch painted lutes.
Or let the prettiest ones
Coax me half-awake. . . .

Drinking with Friends

Tall marsh fowl stalk through the shallows
As little birds nag at the willow buds;

A few wild ducks: puce patterns on gold ground.
Sand on the riverbank is dry and bright

Like our eyes, dry and bright
My friends, our dry, white years!

Eternal yellow sand and sparse white hair,
I ask you what they have to do with Spring?

They come together in the wine-jar, where
We worship all that blooms, all that smells sweet.

Our families? We are bonded to the Court.
The Emperor is our wife, our work, our home.

Ah, we are dry and brilliant, old but strong!
Could *you* learn to seed a furrow, and be free?

Drinking There Alone

I perch on the riverbank, forgetting to go back,
Gaze down at the lucent palaces as they slip their moorings.
Another pleasant blur—peach-blossoms, redolent
Of bees and heat, compete with willow blooms:
Which will faint first?
                                        Birds, white and tawny,
Stripe their migrations, warp
And weft of one another's flight.

Abandon me! But leave me a single swallow
And another. And one more. Dear wine, I don't care!
Abandon me, all of you. This world does not suit;
Not a court regular, unfitted for routine. . . .
Well, well, I am demoted, and my dreams also.
I may no longer look forward to Paradise:
The immortal pleasure of being left alone!
For I summoned, too late, my lost young self
When decision was obsolete.

Spring Goes

Petal by petal, the Spring dissolves.
A small wind carries the rest away.
All nature conspires to sadden me,
But gross, unrepentant, I will be gay.

I devour the flowers that yet remain.
I shall not stint myself on wine.
A cock, red-throated, a green-winged hen:
The kingfishers nest in the ruined vine.

The River Pavilion lists in decay.
Beyond these boundaries I see
A grave stone unicorn, adamant;
He leans on a tomb, stares far away.

You natural laws! I take your measure;
Forgetting rank, work, weary days.
I find my nature made for pleasure,
And drink and linger, all at ease.

I Go Too

Each day when Court is over, I skip to the pawnshop,
My nice Spring wardrobe underneath my arm.
Bit by bit, I am drinking up my clothes!
At night I return from the riverbank, quite soused.

Trying not to glance in the taverns—I owe them all—
Slipping past, I reflect on the shortness of life
Especially mine. I'll never see seventy now.
Well, not many do. Who wants to, anyhow?

Saffron butterflies browse deep in flowers;
Dragonflies dint the placid water now and then.
Soothe me, Spring wind! Keep me gentle forever!
Never cross-grained, as Light and Time pass over.

THWARTED

Thwarted, old friend! Here we are, baulked again!
We live at opposite ends of the same lane
But we haven't seen each other for ten whole days.

I returned my Official Horse to the local authorities;
And this road is rotten, like a deliberate plot,
An obstacle race! Now, thanks to my lack of credit

I can't even rent a conveyance, though I still have shoes.
But what if my department-heads caught me afoot?
Taking such risks with protocol, face, future!
You know I'd walk through brambles to get to you.

⸗ ⸗ ⸗

By morning the rain is furious. I'm resigned.
The Spring wind raves as I do, in my sleep.
But I'm deaf to the ring-bell and the bang-drum,
The summons to Court. Next door a lame donkey grazes.

A complaisant neighbor owns him, lends him. Ho!
But I daren't ride the beast in the slick mud,
Not to that slippery Palace! Let them mark me absent.
Life is one long, fragmented, murky episode.

⸗ ⸗ ⸗

I hate getting through the day without a word;
When you hum your heavenly poems I brim with awe,
Nostalgia at the thought of your sweet cadence.

Magnolia petals fall when they have bloomed,
But you and I are overripe, my friend!
How many times have we two not complained

At the high cost of drinking! Even the corner vendor
Puts too high a price on our Illumination.
We can't steep ourselves in Oblivion any more.

High-sounding, isn't it? Come quickly, then,
To my place, for now it just so happens
I've saved enough small change to buy a gallon.

ADVISER TO THE COURT

East of the Palace Gates: Working Late

By the water-clock it's past dawn as the day watch sounds.
Spring banners are being unfurled for the morning
procession.

Officials march back and forth from the Emperor's audience;
Coming away, we break ranks, to wander among the
blossoms.

I turn back towards my office: willow fronds brush my face
As if to veil my yawns. Eyes blurred in the morning mist.

The city walls are moist from snow that has melted
From the high spires. O the fresh odor of wet stone!

Clouds drift among the towers. Alone again,
I burn the draft of another memorandum.

The next time I lift my head I see twilight outside,
Dawn and dusk identical. Time for home, I suppose.

As I amble along on my horse, I hear sleepy cluckings,
The rustle of hay. The chickens are settling down.

To a Brother Official

Sound of the fifth watch! Dawn hastens to obey
The water-clock. Officially, day has begun.
Peach blossoms, bibulous and blushing
From spring wine; on the banners
The embroidery dragons move uneasily
As if warmed into life by the new sun.

High above the Palace, swallows dip
In the light breeze. As you hurry from the audience
The odor of incense lingers in your sleeves.
O your crystalline mind, my friend!
You move as lyrically, as rapidly
As you write poems.

Because we honor two talented generations,
Your father and you, we call your offices
West of the Palace Gate, the Phoenix Pond.

Working All Night in Springtime

When day begins to darken,
Flowers along the wall
Merge into the shadows.
Skyward, the birds chirp softly,
Searching for a roost.

Ten thousand common households
Are illumined by the stars,
But the firmament of Heaven
Is soaking up the moonlight
Of this most brilliant night.

So quiet! I hear keys turning
In gold locks of the Palace doors.
The wind a faint jingle, sounding
Like the horses of importuners,
As they shake their pendants of jade.

I must present a memorial
To the Throne-room, in the morning.
Sleepless here, whether I work or not,
All night I measure the hours
Of all night, in my mind. . . .

End of an Audience

Their sleeves like purple orchids
Two ladies of the court stand by the inner door
Of the Throne-room, ushering courtiers from the chamber.
Incense whirls in the hallways—the Spring wind!
Sun sparks on the flowered robes of a thousand officials.

The water-clock in the tower shows the hour.
I stand close enough to the Prince to see his expression:
His Majesty looks brilliant with joy today!
When I leave the Palace, I collect my colleagues,
Then we pay our respects to the Ministers of State.

Reply to a Friend's Advice

Leaving the audience by the quiet corridors,
Stately and beautiful, we pass through the Palace gates,

Turning in different directions: you go to the West
With the Ministers of State. I, otherwise.

On my side, the willow-twigs are fragile, greening.
You are struck by scarlet flowers over there.

Our separate ways! You write so well, so kindly,
To caution, in vain, a garrulous old man.

On the Way Out

Last year I rejoined the Emperor by this road
When the barbarians swarmed over the Western suburbs.
I'm so far from having recovered from my fear
That shreds of my soul still dangle in the air.

Dangling and wandering, as I am now,
Loyal to the Throne, yet driven away
To a vast, distant province!—surely his Majesty
Could not have intended this. I have been betrayed.

Ruin! As my talent fails, and I grow old.
My steadfastness in trying times has aged me.
I pull on my horse's reins, and, pausing,
Gaze for a final time on the Palace walls.

BANISHMENT

Too Much Heat, Too Much Work

It's the fourteenth of August, and I'm too hot
To endure food, or bed. Steam and the fear of scorpions
Keep me awake. I'm told the heat won't fade with Autumn.

Swarms of flies arrive. I'm roped into my clothes.
In another moment I'll scream down the office
As the paper mountains rise higher on my desk.

O those real mountains to the south of here!
I gaze at the ravines kept cool by pines.
If I could walk on ice, with my feet bare!

Reunion

Joy in this meeting grieves our two white heads
Knowing they greet each other a final time.
We nod through the long night watches, still resenting
The speed with which the candle shrinks and pales.

I dread the hour the Milky Way dries up forever.
Let us fill our cups and drain them, over and over
While we can, before the world returns with dawn
When we blot our eyes, and turn our backs on each other.

A VISIT IN WINTER

TO THE TEMPLE OF HIS MYSTICAL MAJESTY

(*Formerly known as The Grand Infinitesimal Palace*)

Pole star and northern capital: equal as scepter and orb.
Fences march up the hill like troops protecting the city.
The officer-priests are severe, the guards grim and cautious.

The sky of early winter, celadon, not ice-blue,
Matches the roof-tiles which repel the cold.
Sound of a slap! War between tiles and the weather.

All things come together: In the yard, the gilded tower
Celebrates oneness. Doors, painted with mountains and rivers
Merge with the true landscape, which supports them.

Artifice! To concoct realities, reorder the minute universe,
These roof-beams carved with infinite skill
So that the sun and moon revolve around this place.

The deathless plum-tree has tenacious roots,
Strong as the scent of orchids, sturdy as dynasties.
The victim of history, our emperor, master of virtue.

When we toll the names of great painters, begin with Wu
Who moved whole countrysides into this room,
Nourished to gleaming life, in a hot-house for Heaven and
Earth.

Five learnèd men, in procession like elephants,
Heavy, gray, never breaking their close-linked chain;
Then an orderly flight of geese: a thousand pale officials

Follow them, tame civil servants in dragon robes.
The tassels on their ceremonial head-gear
Toss like flames; wind whips the triangular banners.

Great cedars cast their shadows across the temple grounds
In dark diagonals. Pears, early gold, blush now from the
frost.
Hidden by shadows, jade wind-bells move in the eaves:

Their music. The naked, frozen windlass on the well;
Like the silver emperor of Han, immobilized
For a while. The spirit thaws as the old beliefs are revived.

But is the spirit of man hollow as the note of wind-bells,
Or as a great tree, ripe for felling? Indeed, if we are deathless,
Where then is randomness, Art's impulse, true disorder?

TESTAMENT

100 lines from Tu Fu

I come from Tu Ling, an unimportant man,
Only more vulnerable as the years wear on.
To serve my country! I've clung to this mad dream
Without avail, as better men have done.

I bow to hardship whitening my hair,
Old, already spent at forty, I don't care.
When they slam my coffin-lid I shall stay down.
Till then, I will persist, I will endure!

I mourn for my poor people, laboring,
Starving all seasons—I rail against their wrongs.
Though my cloistered fellow-scholars laugh at me
I shall go on pouring out my passionate songs.

I must cleave to the center of life, not the edge of a dream,
Stay with my brilliant Prince, deep in the living stream.
How could one such as I say goodbye to life forever?
Architects, all we need to build a world is here!

* * *

I have cherished dreams of living by the river;
Spindrift days in sun, without a care.
As clover and sunflower lean toward the source of light
I exult in selfhood, assent to my own spirit.

Any infinitesimal ant wants its own burrow.
Why try to be a whale, prey to great waves or the undertow?
Though I learn my own limitations, I can't learn to obey!
Leave me here on earth, to fail again tomorrow.

When I am silent dust, I will persevere.
To emulate the hermit in his cell,
Relinquishing all! I envy his self-control
And drink uncontrollably to celebrate his call.

I will endure, then thud to earth like a bird
Stricken, to the eternal dust. I will persevere!
So I soothe myself by pouring out the wine
And pouring out my grieved and passionate song.

✓ ✓ ✓

I find the grasses dying with the year.
Wind rips open the hedge-rows; the thoroughfare
From the capital is black when I start out,
Midnight at my back—I, perpetual traveler!

I cannot tie my coat, the frost is so severe;
Intractable buckles, and fingers stiff with hoar.
The icy sun arises. Troops on the chill frontier
Gather their spears and banners against the invader.

Armies have trampled this ground so many times
Crags are worn smooth; but music fills the ravines!
I arrive at the Mountains of Li with the morning watch.
Beside the sulfur springs is the Emperor's coach.

A gust of steam smokes in the frigid air.
Echoes of bells and drums and resonant cries!
Soaking voluptuously in the opaque jasper waters
The Imperial ministers loll here, take their ease.

⁊ ⁊ ⁊

The humble and poor are excluded, all their ilk,
Though they are permitted to weave the pure white silk
For the Imperial harem; women full of fear,
Their husbands flogged by greedy courtiers

To extort their exorbitant taxes. Yes, collect the skins
Of miserable men! That's how you serve your King.
Benevolent talents, beware! You will be done in.
It isn't enough simply to love your fellow-man.

What happened to the gold plate on which we used to dine?
Now it decks the boards of the Emperor's rich hangers-on.
But women like goddesses move through the corridors,
Borne on a perfumed wave and swathed in furs.

Incense! You will hear the pensive harp and lute,
Sup on camel-pad broth and nibble rare winter fruit:
Frosty oranges, and little pungent tangerines,
They glow in the hand against warm sable sheens.

When you've gorged, let the wine sour, food to carrion rot!
Fling the meat and drink out of the lacquered gates!
Outside, only steps from plenty, men lie down
To starve, the courtyards littered with their bones.

The span of a woman's arm separates the gilded pillars
Of the Palace from old posts rotten with wind and rain.
On the wild roads the sons of Han lie frozen,
And I, the courtier, freeze with unappeasable pain.

❦ ❦ ❦

So my traces turn to the North, where two streams meet.
I find the ferry-boat moored at another spot.
The western skies dumped lakes upon the land;
Flood-waters rise to meet my outstretched hand.

Is this wet retribution? Will Heaven's Pillars crack?
A myriad river bridges have swept to rack.
One creaking span remains. We travelers crawl across,
Hand clutching hand. Wide river, hear our curse!

In an evil time, I left my wife in a strange house
Remote from the Court. Now I rejoin my spouse.
I'd rather starve at home than feast at Court.
My Beloveds, I have come to share your fate.

I open my door to wailing. In anguish and anger
My cries join theirs: my infant son has died of hunger.
Even the casual neighbors weep, why not a father?
His guardian, useless and broken, ashamed forever.

My own little child has starved, while I wasn't aware
That our fine autumn harvest had made no difference here.
Dear family, we belong to the privileged class.
How then do the poor endure, starved and harassed

Their property seized, themselves dragged off in bonds
To guard a garrison thousands of miles from home?
What of my life, who have never paid a tax,
Hefted a spear, manned a frontier, beaten a drum?

Our land in flood, and my own heart in flood,
These frantic thoughts are rising like the waters
To flow towards you, wounded, oppressed, bereaved,
In desperate love, China, your sons and daughters.

NOTES

The epigraph, from the *Wên-Fu* of Lu Chi, is the translation of Achilles Fang.

The first three poems in the book are written in the style of Po Chü-I. *Hiding Our Love* is modeled on a poem of the Emperor Wu-Ti. *Night Sounds* and *Summer Near the River* are based on themes in the Book of Songs.

The final passage in *A Month in Summer,* in quotes, is from Basho's prose poem on *The Unreal Dwelling* (Genjũan no Fu), as translated by Donald Keene. The earlier episode about Takamaru, the eleven-year-old priest, is taken from Issa's *The Year of My Life,* as translated by Nobuyuki Yuasa.

The poetess mentioned in *Pro Femina* as wearing chiffon over long johns was Sara Teasdale.